Pre-K 5

W0099535

Feelings

Contents

 **Look and put the sticker.**

you

I

fine

good

 Put sticker on the word.

How are you, Mom?

I am fine .

 Ask and say.

 Color and say.

 good

happy fine sad

happy I good you

 fine

good you

happy

fine good

you great

 Look and put the sticker.

how

happy

great

sad

 **Put sticker on the word.**

How are you, Dad?

I am [great] .

 Ask and say.

p. 2

 p. 3

fine

 p. 5

 p. 6

great

 Good work!

 Wonderful work!

 Great effort!

 For working hard!

 Good work!

 Excellent!

 Well done!

 Well done!

 Special award!

Draw the face.

happy

sad

 **Make a face.**

you	I
fine	how

happy	great
sad	good